D1505972

THE POLAR BEAR AND PENGUIN WILL NEVER MEET!
POLAR ANIMALS

By MARK OBLINGER

Illustrated by RYAN WHEATCROFT

CANTATA
LEARNING
MANKATO, MINNESOTA

WWW.CANTATALEARNING.COM

CANTATA LEARNING

MANKATO, MINNESOTA

Published by Cantata Learning
1710 Roe Crest Drive
North Mankato, MN 56003
www.cantatalearning.com

Library of Congress Control Number: 2014956986
978-1-63290-254-2 (hardcover/CD)
978-1-63290-406-5 (paperback/CD)
978-1-63290-448-5 (paperback)

The Polar Bear and Penguin Will Never Meet!: Polar Animals by Mark Oblinger
Illustrated by Ryan Wheatcroft

Book design, Tim Palin Creative
Editorial direction, Flat Sole Studio
Executive musical production and direction, Elizabeth Draper
Music arranged and produced by Mark Oblinger

Printed in the United States of America.

VISIT
WWW.CANTATALEARNING.COM/ACCESS-OUR-MUSIC
TO SING ALONG TO THE SONG

Polar **regions** are the areas around the South Pole and the North Pole. Antarctica is in the south. The Arctic is in the north. They're cold and icy year round. Few plants grow in these areas, and there are no trees. But many animals, such as penguins and polar bears, live there.

Now turn the page, and sing along.

The polar north is home to Arctic hares,
musk ox, snowy owls, and polar bears.

The polar south has penguins that orcas eat.
The polar bear and penguin will never meet.
The polar bear and penguin will never meet.

8

Way down south is Antarctica,
home to seals and the mighty orca.

Neither minds the icy water
with their layers of fatty **blubber**.

9

Penguins are unable to fly,

but through the water they **glide**.

These birds really like each other.
For warmth, they **huddle** together.

The polar north is home to Arctic hares,
musk ox, snowy owls, and polar bears.

The polar south has penguins that orcas eat.

The polar bear and penguin will never meet.

The polar bear and penguin will never meet.

Way up north, where it's cold all day,
Arctic wolves and foxes play.

14

The polar bear **roams** wild and free
and swims through the icy sea.

Many Arctic animals have fur that's white.
Camouflage keeps them out of sight.

Furry coats help them stay snug and warm
in Arctic snow and ice, wind and storm.

Reindeer prance on frozen ground
in the **tundra**, where no trees are found.

Arctic hares snuggle up in their nests.
At hopping, they are the best.

The polar north is home to Arctic hares,

musk ox, snowy owls, and polar bears.

The polar south has penguins that orcas eat.

The polar bear and penguin will never meet.

The polar bear and penguin will never meet.

SONG LYRICS

The Polar Bear and Penguin Will Never Meet!: Polar Animals

The polar north is home to Arctic hares,
musk ox, snowy owls, and polar bears.

The polar south has penguins that orcas eat.
The polar bear and penguin will never meet.
The polar bear and penguin will never meet.

Way down south is Antarctica,
home to seals and the mighty orca.

Neither minds the icy water
with their layers of fatty blubber.

Penguins are unable to fly,
but through the water they glide.

These birds really like each other.
For warmth, they huddle together.

The polar north is home to Arctic hares,
musk ox, snowy owls, and polar bears.

The polar south has penguins that orcas eat.
The polar bear and penguin will never meet.
The polar bear and penguin will never meet.

Way up north, where it's cold all day,
Arctic wolves and foxes play.

The polar bear roams wild and free
and swims through the icy sea.

Many Arctic animals have fur that's white.
Camouflage keeps them out of sight.

Furry coats help them stay snug and warm
in Arctic snow and ice, wind and storm.

Reindeer prance on frozen ground
in the tundra, where no trees are found.

Arctic hares snuggle up in their nests.
At hopping, they are the best.

The polar north is home to Arctic hares,
musk ox, snowy owls, and polar bears.

The polar south has penguins that orcas eat.
The polar bear and penguin will never meet.
The polar bear and penguin will never meet.

The Polar Bear and Penguin Will Never Meet!: Polar Animals

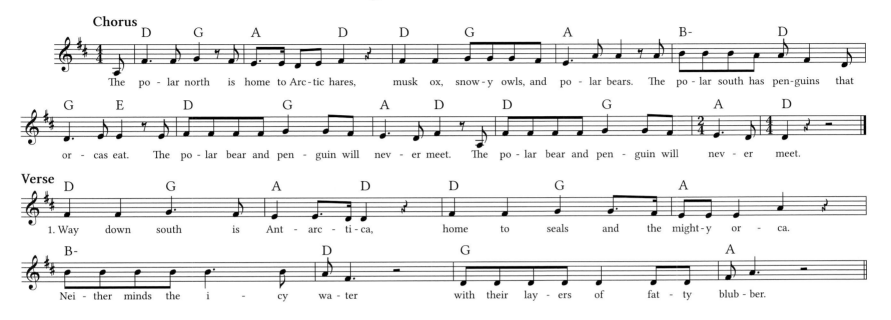

Chorus

The po-lar north is home to Arc-tic hares, musk ox, snow-y owls, and po-lar bears. The po-lar south has pen-guins that or - cas eat. The po-lar bear and pen - guin will nev - er meet. The po-lar bear and pen-guin will nev - er meet.

Verse

1. Way down south is Ant - arc - ti - ca, home to seals and the might-y or - ca. Nei - ther minds the i - cy wa - ter with their lay - ers of fat - ty blub - ber.

Verse 2
Penguins are unable to fly,
but through the water they glide.
These birds really like each other.
For warmth, they huddle together.

Verse 3
Way up north, where it's cold all day,
Arctic wolves and foxes play.
The polar bear roams wild and free
and swims through the icy sea.

Verse 4
Many Arctic animals have fur that's white.
Camouflage keeps them out of sight.
Furry coats help them stay snug and warm
in Arctic snow and ice, wind and storm.

Chorus

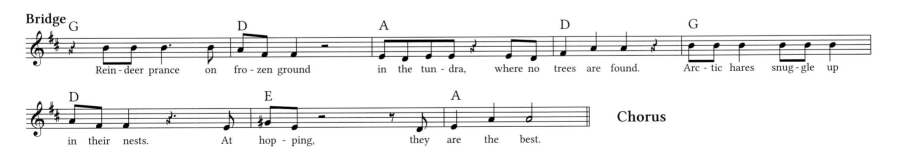

Bridge

Rein - deer prance on fro - zen ground in the tun - dra, where no trees are found. Arc - tic hares snug - gle up in their nests. At hop - ping, they are the best.

Chorus

GLOSSARY

blubber—a layer of fat that keeps penguins, whales, and seals warm in icy water

camouflage—coloring that helps animals hide in their natural surroundings

glide—to move smoothly and easily

huddle—to come close together

regions—large areas

roams—wanders

tundra—frozen land where few plants and no trees grow

GUIDED READING ACTIVITIES

1. Who is the author of this book? Why do you think he picked the title *The Polar Bear and Penguin Will Never Meet*?

2. How are penguins and polar bears different? How are they the same?

3. Pick your favorite animal in this book. How is it able to survive in a polar region?

TO LEARN MORE

Amstutz, Lisa J. *Polar Animal Adaptations*. Mankato, MN: Capstone, 2012.

Hall, Katharine. *Polar Bears and Penguins: A Compare and Contrast Book*. Mount Pleasant, SC: Sylvan Dell, 2014.

Hynes, Margaret. *Polar Lands*. London: Kingfisher-Macmillan Children's, 2012.

Waldron, Melanie. *Polar Regions*. Chicago: Raintree, 2013.